CONTENTS

LIST OF MAPS

Maps   **Page**

CHAPTER 1

HISTORICAL SETTING

Introduction

It is a truism that Syria's intervention in the Lebanese Civil War resulted in sending over 40,000 troops into Lebanon between 1975 and 1976. Most of these troops remain there to this day. While the prevailing thought is that this intervention helped end the fighting and bloodshed between Lebanon's recalcitrant sectarian factions, it is increasingly clear that this came at a high political and military cost for Damascus. This essay will argue that contradictory Syrian strategic objectives coupled with a mismatch between Syria's strategic interests and its military operations, and a misapplication of military force prolonged the conflict in Lebanon, and were in part responsible for the high cost of sustaining Syria's military credibility and guarantee as a peacemaker. This paper will develop the above argument by (1) analyzing Syria's strategic, operational, and tactical objectives in Lebanon between 1975-1976, (2) showing how the misapplication of Syrian military force in Lebanon hindered Damascus's ability to achieve long term strategic gains, and (3) showing how the Syrian experience in Lebanon could be useful in avoiding similar future pitfalls for US commanders, warfighters, and warplanners.

Historical Setting

When the Lebanese Civil War broke out in 1975, Syrian President Hafiz al-Assad had been in power for a tumultuous five years, experiencing events both domestically and internationally that threatened his new regime. While able to remain in power and even

1

expand his influence during that period, the constant pressure upon his regime made the President fully aware of the need for some stability to consolidate his power and institute his vision of Syria. Assad's experiences during his rise to the Presidency and the early years of his reign heavily influenced his vision of Syria, its regional role, and set the stage for his decision to invade Lebanon. To fully understand his decision, a brief description of the strategic setting from Syria's domestic and international viewpoint is required.

Two main domestic factors were responsible for Assad's decision to send troops into Lebanon: the Ba'th Party and Assad's Alawi religious affiliation. The Ba'th party had consolidated power in the 1960's with Hafiz Assad as one of the primary power players in the rise of the party. Undergoing internal changes throughout the sixties, by the time Assad rose to power, the underlying philosophy of the party could be summed up as a socialist, non-sectarian ideology with a pan-Arabic vision. But that very ideology created tension in the domestic power bases within the country.

With a socialist vision, Ba'th agendas such as land reform and social justice quite naturally alienated much of the ruling elite. Its appeal was to those groups that felt they were left behind economically, largely the rural populace.[1] Thus when Assad took power in a bloodless coup in 1970, he was faced with internal dissention between the old ruling elite in the cities and those largely rural elements of society that had been economically less fortunate. Once in power, he strove to reconcile those groups to bring stability to his regime.

---

[1]   LT Mark A Huber, USN, *Legitimacy and Hafez Al-Asad*, Naval Postgraduate School Thesis (Monterey, CA: Naval Postgraduate School, June, 1992), 21

Breaking with the harsh socialism of the Ba'thist party of the Sixties, Assad made great strides in changing the party to reflect a more centrist view. As author Patrick Seale states, Assad

> knew he needed allies in the urban middle class, so, breaking with his political past, he tried to win over the shopkeepers, businessmen, and artisans of the towns as well as the many citzens who had fled Syria since 1963, mainly Sunnis from the former leading families.[2]

By canceling many of the planned land reforms and wooing the middle class, Assad made strides in consolidating his power.

But Assad did not abandon the rural sector nor all of the fundamental ideals of Ba'th party. He instituted many less severe social welfare programs that gained him a solid acceptance amongst many sectors in society. Food prices were cut by 15 percent and responsibility for criminal prosecution was turned over to the police instead of the army.[3] Assad also instituted local governmental bodies to provide local outlets for regional disputes. These efforts paid off in keeping dissention under control. But Assad's second domestic crisis would soon appear when a new constitution was proposed.

In January 1973, the new constitution was proposed by Assad. The constitution failed to stipulate that the President was required to be a Muslim, nor did it stipulate Islam as the national religion. Protests, largely by Sunni Muslims, took place throughout the country. Assad gave in to the protests, adding the requirement for the President to be a Muslim, but stood firm against the national religion issue. While this should have been no major problem, Assad was an Alawi, considered by many Sunni Muslims as a

---

[2]   Patrick Seale, *ASAD of Syria: The Struggle for the Middle East* (London: I. B. Tauris & Co Ltd, 1988), 171.

[3]   Seale, 171.

heterodox form of Islam.[4] If Assad was not a Muslim, he could not be President. Assad asked the Lebanese Shi'i Imam Musa al-Sadr to issue a *Fatwa* confirming Alawis as a Shi'a sect.[5] Although this action averted the immediate crisis, the tension between Alawi and Sunni Muslims would remain an issue.

Assad was faced with considerable social and political pressures that tended to make his regime seem fragile. Above all, his strategic goals would have to be pursued with these social tensions and regime survival in mind. Internationally, the strategic setting has to be viewed with the Syrian domestic tensions in mind.

Internationally, by far the most significant events to form Assad's vision of Syria's future were the defeats by the Israelis in 1967 and 1973. Having been deeply affected by the humiliating defeat and loss of the Golan Heights in 1967, Hafiz Assad began planning for military action to take back the heights and force Israeli concessions immediately upon seizing power in 1970. To do so, he needed to rearm and forge alliances against Israel. To rearm, he turned to the Soviet Union where he made several personal trips early in his presidency.[6] Through his diplomacy, he was able to gain the arms necessary to strike at his enemy in the October War of 1973.

Among the Arab nations, Assad turned to Egypt's Anwar Sadat for an ally. Sadat, for his own reasons, agreed to military action against the Israelis, although his goals in the conflict were largely at odds with Syria's, a fact that Sadat kept secret from his ally. In short, Sadat's aims were never to make more than a token show of force,

---

[4]   Seale, 173. For more information on Alawis see appendix A.

[5]   Seale, 173.

[6]   Seale, 175.

establishing a beachhead on the Sinai and force Israel to bargain for peace with terms suitable to Egypt's interests. The resulting defeat of the Arab forces set the stage for American duplicity that served to isolate Syria further.[7]

Among Syria's other neighbors, Jordan and Iraq, Assad could not hope for any military partnership with whom to threaten Israel and gain back the territory lost in 1967. Traditional rivals, there was no love lost between Damascus and Baghdad. After the loss in 1973, in fact, the bad blood between Syria and her neighbor increased. To the south, Jordan and Syria formed a bond of necessity, but of no military value. At best, Syria could only hope that Jordan would provide protection on her south from any Israeli invasion along that access, but would not be of any offensive help.

So on the eve of civil war in Lebanon, Syria found herself isolated militarily, having been betrayed by Sadat, who was moving towards the Sinai II agreement and eventual reconciliation with Israel. Domestically, Assad felt marginally secure, but fully aware that sectarian feuds, Israeli intervention, or intrigue from Iraq could threaten the survival of his regime. With this strategic background, we turn now to Syrian strategic goals and their relationship to Assad's decision to intervene in Lebanon.

---

[7]   Seale, 189-20. For more background information see Seale, Chapter 14.

CHAPTER 2

SYRIAN STRATEGIC GOALS

In the United States' military, warfare is defined at three levels: tactical, operational, and strategic. At the lowest end, the tactical level is primarily the realm of the military warfighters. The tactical level of war is defined by battles between combatants. As such, it answers the "how" of warfighting. At the next level, the operational level of war involves the planning of campaigns and actions to support national strategic aims. As such, it is primarily the realm of the military warplanners. The operational level of war is critical to tying military actions to a strategic end, and answers the "what" of warfighting. At the highest level, the strategic level of war involves national policy and objectives. It is largely the realm of politicians and policy makers. The strategic level of war is the most critical, for it answers the "why" of warfighting, without which tactical and operational actions are without purpose.

History is replete with examples of great tactical and operational level successes that ultimately failed to achieve a strategic goal. The Germans in World War Two were tremendous tacticians and campaign fighters, but strategically failed. They won many great victories, yet lost the war in the end due to failed strategy. Likewise, the Americans in the Vietnam War were tremendously successful on the battlefield, yet lost the war. The strategy of building a democratic nation in South Vietnam was arguably not achievable by military force. As will be shown, the Syrians failed in Lebanon due to poor strategy.

On 13 April, 1975, a bus load of armed Palestinian gunmen was ambushed in the Ayn-Rummaneh district of Beirut, killing twenty seven people. This bloodshed sparked the civil war that would lead to Syrian military involvement in Lebanon on a scale that would not diminish to the present. With an understanding of the internal weakness and military isolation of Syria in 1975, we can look now at the strategic goals that drove Assad to intervene in Lebanon. Hafiz Assad's had five strategic goals in Lebanon, including: (1) Prevention of a radical regime led by the National Movement from gaining power in Lebanon; (2) Securing the Syrian western flank from Israeli invasion; (3) Controlling the Palestinian Liberation Organization (PLO); (4) Gaining legitimacy as the leader of pan-Arabism following the death of Nasser, and; (5) Enhancing the prospect of a "Greater Syria."

As has already been shown, many within his country did not fully accept Assad's Alawi regime. His power base was strong, but narrowly focused.[8] Strong support for Assad existed in the army, which was his strategic center of gravity, and among the rural population that benefited most from the Ba'th policies. But Assad faced opposition from some of the old ruling Sunni elite who had lost the most power since the rise of the Ba'th Party. Additionally, among many conservative Muslims, the Alawis remained outside of the Islamic world. Radical groups like the Moslem Brotherhood found Assad's Alawi religion ripe grounds for dissention.[9]

---

[8]   CDR John C. Burch, USN, *BackGround Issues Concerning Soviet Foreign Policy and Syrian Initiatives in the Middle East*, Naval Post Graduate Thesis, (Monterey, CA: Naval PostGraduate School, March 1986), 29.

[9]   Seale, 178.

With internal weaknesses at home, and feeling isolated at large, the eruption of violence in Lebanon posed a threat to Hafiz Assad that could not be ignored. Syria and Lebanon enjoyed a symbiotic relationship, not surprising since Lebanon had been splintered from Syria under the French Mandate. The ties between the countries were indisputable. As Patrick Seale states, "The two countries were like connecting vessels: the political temperature of the one could not but affect that of the other."[10] Thus, violence in one country affected the other. When the radical National Movement, backed by PLO forces began to seriously threaten the stability of Lebanon, Assad had to act for stability at home. He could not afford a radical movement along his borders that could spillover into Syria.

The second strategic goal was securing Syria's western flank against Israeli invasion. In 1973, the Israeli's had come within 25 miles of Damascus, a lesson not soon forgotten. Southern Lebanon provided a route for Israel to flank existing Syrian defensive forces arrayed against Israeli positions on the Golan Heights. The Bekaa Valley in particular provided a dangerous avenue of approach should Israel decide to once again conduct offensive actions against Syria (See Map 1). The possibility of permanently closing off that route was a major consideration for Assad.

Assad faced another quandary. As the fighting in Lebanon increased and the Christians began to be hard pressed by the PLO and National Movement, the specter of Israeli intervention in Lebanon became stronger. He could not possibly sit by and do nothing if Israel invaded Lebanon for fear of the reaction at home. Yet he was not

---

[10]   Seale, 269.

8

militarily strong enough to take on the Israelis alone. Assad had to preempt Israeli action, or suffer the prospect of losing power.

Syria's third strategic objective, was to gain control over the PLO in Lebanon. Syria's relations with the PLO had been mixed since Yasser Arafat's rise to prominence. While ardent supporters of the Palestinian cause, Syria saw their cause as linked to that of the Arab people, not strictly the Palestinians. From 1964-1966, Palestinian units, supported and led by Syrians, operated against Israel, often using the Golan area as an infiltration point. But the Syrians closely controlled the military operations and Arafat had chafed under the tight controls placed on his group.

Yasser Arafat saw the Palestinian cause as one of the Palestinian people.[11] While he needed Arab support, he desired to lead the effort to regain Palestine unfettered by any authority, feeling it was up to the Palestinians to achieve their objectives on terms of their own choosing. If he allowed other nations to dictate the conditions upon which the PLO were to operate, the objectives of the PLO would be in danger of being subordinate to the strategic objectives of the sponsoring state, as it had been earlier while operating from Jordan and Syria.

While in Syria, Arafat had conducted unsanctioned operations, earning him the wrath of Hafiz Assad, then Minister of Defense and responsible for all military actions. In May 1966, the leader of the PLF was found murdered and Assad, suspecting Arafat, threw him in jail for 55 days. Arafat was finally released on the terms that he would never return.[12] Thus, Arafat and Assad had historical differences, and when the PLO were

---

[11]   Ghada H. Talhami, *Syria and the Palestinians* (Gainesville, FL: University Press of Florida, 2001), 149.

[12]   Talhami,, 85-87.

later evicted from Jordan after trying to overthrow the government, they moved their operating base to Beirut instead of Damascus in the hopes of operating independent of state sponsorship. This very independence could threaten Syria's own long-term objectives regarding Israel. If Arafat decided to make peace with the Israelis on his own terms, Syria could not tie that peace to his own objective of regaining the Golan Heights. Consequently, Assad desired to reign in an independent PLO.

Another reason for Assad's desire to gain control of the PLO was the destabilizing influence they were having in Lebanon. Uncontrolled operations against Israel were being answered by increasingly violent retaliatory strikes in Lebanon. Between 1968-1974, the Israelis conducted forty-four major retaliatory strikes against PLO positions in Lebanon. [13] Assad was convinced that the Israeli's were using the PLO incursions as a reason to fragment the Lebanese society. Palestinian actions and the Lebanese Army's inability to stop them was increasingly driving a wedge between the Christians, who thought they should be punished, and the Muslims, who thought the PLO should be protected. As Seale states

> If the Christians were driven by Palestinian and Muslim pressure to set up a sectarian statelet of their own, Arab nationalism…would be discredited, Islam would be made to seem intolerant, the Palestinian program for a 'secular democratic state' embracing Muslims, Christians and Jews would appear hollow, and Israel would reign supreme over the balkanized Levant. [14]

In fact, the prospect of a Christian drive for a separate mini-state was very real. By late 1975, the primary Christian leaders, Camille Chamoun, Suleiman Faranjiyaa, and Bashir Jumayyil, began to talk openly about the possibility of a Christian retraction to the

---

[13]   Seale, 275.

[14]   Seale, 275.

pre-1920 boundaries centered on Mount Lebanon. Increased Palestinian support of the National Movement convinced the Phalangists that a return to *status quo* was unattainable without foreign intervention. [15] Whether it was political rhetoric or a true desire upon the part of the Christians to create an autonomous canton within Lebanon, to Syria, the prospect of a separate, pro-Western entity in Lebanon was patently unacceptable. In Assad's eyes, it would create a "Maronite Zion" in the middle of the country. [16] PLO involvement in the conflict was therefore upsetting the precarious balance in Lebanon, creating potential problems for Syria. To meet his own goals, then, Assad needed to gain control of the PLO.

Assad's fourth strategic objective was to gain prominence as the new leader of pan-Arabism. As a cornerstone of the Ba'th platform, pan-Arabism was a secular ideal that crossed sectarian lines. Between 1958-1961, Syria had joined with Egypt to form the short-lived United Arab Republic. [17] Led by the pan-Arabic ideals of Gamal Abdul Nasser, Assad had served in Egypt during the UAR period and was heavily influenced by his experience there. But Nasser had died in 1970, and pan-Arabism remained without a strong central figure. Assad considered Syria the natural successor to the pan-Arabic movement, and frequently used the pan-Arabic message in news releases and speeches. [18]

---

[15]   Rabinovich, 47.

[16]   Itamar Rabinovich, *The War for Lebanon 1970-1983* (Ithaca, NY: Cornell University Press, 1984) 47.

[17]   Talhami, 57-58.

[18]   Huber, 31-39. Huber quotes several press releases that signify the use of pan-Arabism as a central theme.

In his thesis written at the Naval Postgraduate School, LT Mark Huber, USN,[19] makes a convincing argument that Assad's support of pan-Arabic ideals was disingenuous. His thesis is that pan-Arabism was only a tool used by Assad to add legitimacy to his regime. He points out the fact that Syria backed non-Arab Iran against Arab Iraq in their eight-year war. Whether his thesis is correct or not is largely irrelevant. The fact is that Assad wanted to be viewed as the leader of pan-Arabism whether his commitment to its ideals was real or not. In his landmark radio speech to the Syrian people on July 20, 1976, Assad stated

> On our position on Lebanon, we proceed from the fact that we are sons of a single Arab nation. What prompts us to show serious concern toward what is happening in Lebanon is our anxiety over the tragedies there. We are concerned about all Lebanese---Christians and Moslems---because they are the sons of our Arab nation and come under the flag of Arab nationalism.[20]

In regards to Lebanon, Assad clearly used the pan-Arabic argument to justify his actions there, whether his beliefs were genuine or not.

Assad's final, and perhaps most debatable, strategic goal was the possibility of gaining control over Lebanon and bringing back a splintered province of "Greater Syria" into the fold. Up until 1975, Syria had been unable to concentrate efforts on gaining back territory severed by the French, although they had influenced events in Lebanon to a certain degree. The instability at home, frequent coups, and continued tensions with Israel all tended to delay any serious efforts to incorporate Lebanon. Ever the opportunist, Assad saw a possibility growing as events unfolded in the neighboring conflict.

---

[19]   Huber, 31-39.

[20]   Rabinovich, 215.

That Syria saw Lebanon and Palestine as an integral part of her is hard to dispute.

Pertaining to Palestine, Assad told Yasser Arafat

> You do not represent Palestine as much as we do. Do not forget one thing:
> there is no Palestinian people, no Palestinian entity, there is only Syria!
> You are an integral part of the Syrian people and Palestine is an integral
> part of Syria. Therefore it is we, the Syrian authorities, who are the real
> representatives of the Palestinian people.[21]

This statement unveils Assad's view of a "Greater Syria." In Lebanon, the feelings of

unity went even deeper.

Despite three agreements to the contrary, Syria has yet to remove its military

occupation force from Lebanon. The continued Syrian presence has affected virtually

every facet of Lebanese life. In the words of international lawyer and human rights

advocate Muhammed Mugraby,

> Official Syrian holidays, such as the one commemorating Assad's
> "Correctional Movement," are celebrated in Lebanon as in Syria. Pictures
> of Hafiz al Assad and his sons…greet passengers at the Beirut airport
> much as they do at the Damascus airport. Lebanese newspapers and
> media carry no criticism of Syrian policies, either explicitly or implicitly.[22]

Moreover, the influx of hundreds of thousands of Syrian workers in Lebanon, who are

allowed to settle there and sometimes bring family members, has contributed to a steady

remaking of Lebanon into a lesser Syrian state.[23] This view of Lebanon as part of Syria is

reflected in political rhetoric from Damascus, which has "…made innumerable claims to

Lebanon and uses such terms as 'brotherly' relations between two 'statelets.'[24]

---

[21]   Huber, 42.

[22]   Muhammed Mugraby, "Lebanon, a Wholly Owned Subsidiary," *Middle East Quarterly*, March 1998, 12.

[23]   Daniel Pipes, "We Don't Need Syria in Lebanon," *Middle East Quarterly,* September 2000, 21-23.

[24]   Habib C. Malik, "Is There Still a Lebanon?" *Middle East Quarterly*, December, 1997, 18.

Beyond the social changes resulting from Syria's involvement in Lebanon, the Lebanese government is totally subservient to Syria. Politicians from Beirut travel frequently to Damascus to "consult" with the Syrian leadership. Syrian backed political candidates are elected, sometimes through outright fraud. One example of this political interference on the part of the Syrians was the declaration by the Lebanese parliament of Rafiq al-Harari as the Prime Minister in 1998. Harari, Syria's choice, had renounced his Lebanese citizenship and lived in Saudi Arabia. Consequently, he had no political credentials as a legitimate Lebanese candidate. Yet Syrian influence ensured his election.[25]

Finally, Syria has moved to economically tie the two countries closer than ever. Lebanon was forced to convert their power stations to liquefied natural gas, which is provided by Syria. Common power grids and roads have been forced on the Lebanese people, tying the two countries together.[26] Construction contracts are given to companies chosen by the Syrian proxies in Beirut,[27] and many of the construction workers are Syrians.[28] Lebanon has provided a protected market for cheap Syrian goods, which are dumped on the market to the detriment of the Lebanese economy.[29] The result is an integrated economy, which has not only benefited Syria, but created long term dependence by Lebanon on continued Syrian ties. Continued Syrian military presence, political manipulation by Damascus to shape the Lebanese government in their favor,

---

[25]   Mugraby, 12.

[26]   Pipes, 22-23.

[27]   Mugabry, 14. Harari awarded one of his own companies concession over the entire old city of Beirut.

[28]   Malik, 18.

existence of hundreds of thousands of Syrian workers, and creation of long term economic ties are all clear anecdotal evidence that integrating Lebanon was one of Assad's objectives.

Understanding Assad's five strategic goals, we can now turn to the operational and tactical levels of war. The problems Assad faced implementing his vision, and the elements of power he used are instructive to us as warfighters.

---

[29] Pipes, 23.

CHAPTER 3

OPERATIONAL AND TACTICAL OBJECTIVES

To analyze Assad's operational and tactical objectives, it is useful to look at the war in four phases as defined by author Itamar Rabinovich. The first, from April through June, 1975, is viewed as a transition between the traditional sectarian outbreaks of violence that were more or less commonplace, to a full scale civil war. The second, from June 1975 to January 1976 covers the war before Syrian military intervention. The third, from January through May, 1976 is Syrian intervention prior to invasion. The last phase from May to October, 1976, covers the Syrian invasion and war settlement.[30] These divisions provide a useful framework for capturing the essence of the Syria's operational and tactical level involvement in the conflict.

Phase I-Transition

After the ambush of the Palestinians, violence between competing factions broke out in Beirut and Tripoli. In Beirut, the Phalangist Christians, joined by other minor parties, clashed with the PLO. The Christians were fighting to maintain their dominance, and their way of life in the city. The Palestinians were fighting to maintain the hard fought freedom of action they had gone to Lebanon for in the first place.[31]

---

[30]   Rabinovich, 43-49.

[31]   Rabinovich, 44.

In Tripoli, the conflict arose between Christian supporters of President Faranjiyya and supporters of Rashid Karami, influential Sunni leader of the city. Karami, possibly settling a score for Suleiman Faranjiyya's rebuffing an earlier attempt to make power sharing concessions with the Sunni elite, no more wanted a civil war than did the Christians.[32] Reform to give the Sunni's more power was his goal, but any war that unleashed radical elements was detrimental to the ruling Sunnis as much as the Christians. The fighting in Beirut, while bloody, was nothing out the ordinary by Lebanese standards, particularly in the early 1970's.

Two events transformed the war from a short skirmish to a bloody civil war. First, Kamal Jumblatt, the Druze leader who had organized the reformists under a loose umbrella called the National Movement, called for the removal of Phalangists from the Cabinet.[33] This caused a walkout of the Christian Ministers and a collapse of the government. Second, the deep-rooted feelings of mistrust between the various sects had risen to the point where reconciliation had become nearly impossible.

Assad's operational goal during this phase was to end the conflict and increase Syrian ability to influence events in the Lebanese government.. The collapse of the government prompted Syria to begin shaping actions. For Syria, these actions were diplomatic, not military. On May 24, Assad sent his foreign minister, 'Abd al-Halim Khaddam, and vice defense minister, Naji Jamil, to mediate in the crisis.[34] President Faranjiyya had tried to resolve the growing crisis by appointing a reserve officer to the

---

[32]   William W. Harris, *Faces of Lebanon* (Princeton, NJ: Markus Weiner Publishers, 1996), 160.

[33]   Talhami, 113.

[34]   Marius Deeb, *The Lebanese Civil* War (New York, NY: Praeger Publishers, 1980) 5.

position of Prime Minister, and seven other officers and one civilian to create a cabinet. This not only failed, but the appointment of a military cabinet further provoked the Sunni and Shi'i communities.[35] President Faranjiyya, upon Syrian urgings, asked Rashid Karami to accept the post of Prime Minister and form a government. Initially unable to do so, the Syrians again intervened. On June 16-17 and June 29, Khaddam and the Syrian Army Chief of Staff traveled to Lebanon and negotiated with key leaders from the government and communal groups to form a "government of communal balance." By the end of June, the cabinet was formed. But it was too late. The situation had deteriorated to the point where phase two, all out war, was imminent.[36]

Phase II- War

A level of violence heretofore unknown in the country characterized phase two. After two months of low levels of violence, fighting again broke out in September. While retaining much of the sectarian nature of earlier conflicts, the inclusion of the PLO[37] and violence across the entire country instead of the usual localized conflicts changed the nature of the conflict. The PLO's goal in the conflict was not the reform of Lebanon. They fought to maintain control of the refugee camps which were the source of their strength, and their tenuous hold in Beirut. For the most part the PLO remained in a defensive role to protect their positions.

---

[35]   Harris, 161.

[36]   Rabinovich, 44.

[37]   Rabinovich, 47. Understanding that the PLO was not the unified group it later became, the term PLO is used here for simplicity to mean the major Palestinian groups who eventually sided and fought with the leftist Muslim groups. As in all things in Lebanon, nothing is as easy as it seems.

The conflict soon spread throughout the country, concentrated around cities. Beirut, Tripoli, Zahle, and Akkar all became battlefields.[38] In Beirut, Christian militias overran the Muslim section of Karatina, which separated East Beirut from the port. A massacre of Palestinians and Shi'i followed. To the south, the Christian town of Damour was decimated by Muslim forces, killing hundreds of Christians, and once cleansed, became a Palestinian stronghold.[39]

Syrian reaction to the escalation of fighting was once again diplomatic. The scope and target of the shaping action changed, however. On the Lebanese front, Khaddam met in September and October with the Lebanese leaders to try once again to diffuse the situation. While some reforms were tried, they were much too little and too late for any effect on the war. Among the changes were allocating more power to the Prime Minister and reducing the power of the President; allowing the control of the army to pass to the Prime Minister; and deciding to allow the Lebanese Army, which had remained out of the fighting, to intervene in the crisis.[40] The Army's intervention, however, had no impact on the conflict, and the mild reforms were much too insignificant to placate the mood of the combatants.

Assad also used his diplomatic skills to prevent potential rivals from influencing events in Lebanon. Largely successful, it did not keep other Arab nations completely out of the crisis. Libya, Iraq, and Saudi Arabia all attempted to influence events at one time or another. To allow other countries to participate in the conflict would undermine the

---

[38]   Rabinovich, 49.

[39]   Harris, 162.

[40]   Rabinovich, 46-47.

Syrian's strategic goals, however, and Assad quickly blocked any significant interference with his efforts. In essence, Assad used his diplomatic skills to not only shape the Lebanese government to his liking, but to isolate the battlefield from other participants.

As he was unable to obtain his operational goals via diplomacy alone, Assad decided to militarily intervene in the war. Up until this point, his goal had been to support the revisionist bloc through attempted reforms, while preventing them from gaining too much influence. He realized that continuing to support the revisionists on one hand, and then using diplomatic means to try and influence the outcome along status quo lines, was not working and had little chance of future success.[41]

Phase III-Initial Military Intervention

Phase three of the war, the intervention by Syria, is perhaps the most interesting. It began with intervention on behalf of the traditional allies, the Muslim reformists, but quickly turned into support for the Maronite status quo bloc. This remarkable turn of events can only be understood by examining Syria's operational goals.

Assad's operational objective during Phase III was to pressure the Christian militia to the point of accepting Syrian sponsored compromises supportive of his goals. He saw Christian strongholds around Beirut, Zahle, Deir al-Qamar, and Zgharta as key tactical targets. Strongholds adjacent to Beirut, such as Damour, could block PLO forces from the south, and Assad at this time wanted to use the PLO forces against the Christians. Zahle threatened freedom of movement along the critical Beirut/Damascus Highway. Deir al-Qamar was the hometown of Cammille Chamoun, and Zgharta the

---

[41]   Rabinovich, 47-48.

hometown of President Franjiyya. By tactically applying pressure to these population centers, then, Assad could directly attack the centers of gravity for the Christians, their key family group leaders, enable the PLO to move north, and open the Beirut-Damascus Highway. He did not want to destroy the Christians, but rather, by pressing hard at these targets, to shape the political face of Lebanon in his favor. In essence, he wanted to create a pro-Syrian regime, enabling him to pursue his long-range strategic objectives.[42]

But the Syrian leader had significant challenges to overcome before he could risk overt military involvement in the crisis. First, he had to ensure the Israeli's would not intervene, yet it was clear that any military moves into Lebanon would be a cause for Israel to strike.[43] Second, he had to gain American acceptance of Syrian actions. And finally, he had to keep good relations with his powerful allies the Soviets. Yet he desperately needed to send in military forces push achieve his agenda.

Israel, through the United States ambassador to Syria, Richard Murphy, had conveyed to Assad that Israel would view any Syrian military action in Lebanon as a significant threat to their own security. Murphy went on to say that "…the United States might not be able to hold Israel back."[44] With the loss of Egypt as a potential ally to threaten Israel's border, and Jordan unwilling to face the Zionists again, Assad would risk facing the Israeli military alone if he sent Syrian forces into Lebanon. Syria would be vastly overmatched. Therefore, a prerequisite for Syrian actions in Lebanon was prior Israeli acceptance.

---

[42] Farid El Khazen, *The Breakdown of the State of Lebanon 1967-1976* (Cambridge, MA: 2000) 325-327.

[43] Seale, 278.

[44] Seale, 278.

21

American acceptance was nearly as critical as Israel's. The American's had intervened before in 1958. It was possible that they would again. Moreover, Assad was convinced that the Americans and Israelis were inciting the Phalangists to fight against the Palestinians.[45] Israel would follow the United States' direction, making American acceptance of Syrian military intervention as crucial as Israel's.

Finally, his Soviet benefactors were decidedly against any action in Lebanon. They were sympathetic to Kamal Jumblatt's left wing National Movement, with which they were in ideological agreement.[46] Moreover, they had ties with Arafat and the PLO. They saw potential gain in extending their regional influence through a clear left wing victory. Assad needed Soviet arms and influence to counteract western strength, but his goals in Lebanon conflicted with theirs.

While contemplating what to do about the obstacles to his objectives, Assad decided against intervention by regular Syrian forces. Instead, he utilized Sa'iqa and the Palestine Liberation Army (PLA), which were both Syrian units made up of Palestinians.[47] By doing so, he could minimize the risk of American-Israeli reaction, claiming these were simply Palestinians, not Syrians. By sending these forces to fight against the Christians, he hoped to bring a swift end to the fighting and force the Christians to accept a compromise favorable to Syrian objectives. This would satisfy his Soviet backers, prevent Jumblatt from creating a radical regime, and maintain a form of the status quo desired by the Christians.

---

[45]   Seale, 276.

[46]   Seale. 286. Jumblatt had even been awarded the Lenin Peace Prize.

[47]   Khazen, 325-326. Sa'iqa was a PLO guerilla unit under the control of Syria. The PLA was a regular Syrian Army brigade made up of Palestinians and led by Syrian officers.

On the second week of January 1976, these elements entered the war. Fighting alongside the PLO and the reformists, the additional forces pressed the Christians hard. Sa'iqa in particular was instrumental in seizing Damour, which proved a key setback for the Christian forces. Tactically, the Syrian backed forces would cut off major supply routes to an area, surround the city, and rely heavily on artillery preparation fire to cause extensive damage. After sufficient preparation, they would attack on multiple fronts to clear the town. In this case, the entire population left and it became a PLO stronghold.[48]

While militarily pressing the status quo forces, Assad pressed the Lebanese government to accept a cease-fire, with conditions dictated by the Syrians favorable to the reformists, and to Syria. On February 7, President Faranjiyya agreed to the conditions, and publicly reaffirmed the conditions of the Cairo agreement, which essentially gave the PLO autonomy in Southern Lebanon. The publication of the Reform Document followed, which had four provisions. First, it further limited the power of the President while guaranteeing a Christian position. Second, it limited the confessional system. Third, it promised social reforms. And finally, it hinted at changes to citizenship laws that would possibly include the Palestinians at some future date.[49]

The status quo bloc found the reforms acceptable in light of the alternatives available to them. The reformists, particularly Kamal Jumblatt, along with the PLO rejected its provisions for different reasons. The reforms were not far reaching enough for the radical Jumblatt, who rejected what he considered minor reforms. His goal was nothing less than a complete elimination of the confessional system of government and

---

[48]   Khazen, 332.

[49]   Rabinovich, 50.

institution of a secular one. The PLO rejected any hint of Syrian presence. After all, they

had come to Lebanon to gain freedom of action from Syria and the other conservative

Arab regimes.[50] Before he could try something else, Assad faced new challenges.

In late January, a Muslim army officer, Lt Ahmed al-Khatib, supported with

Libyan finances and orchestrated by Arafat's Fatah leader, Abu Jihad, defected and

formed the Lebanese Arab Army(LAA). The LAA successfully took over several

barracks and gained in popularity. On March 11, Brigadier 'Aziz al-Ahdab, backed by

Abu Hassan Salemeh, another Arafat associate, announced a coup against the President.

The Muslims demanded his resignation, but the Syrians refused to let him leave until his

successor was elected. This rebellion against Syrian interests convinced Assad of PLO

complicity.[51] The disintegration of the Lebanese army and Khatib's rise, praised by

Jumblatt and Arafat, were met with Syrian displeasure as described by foreign minister

Khaddam that if

> Ahmad al-Khatib is not ended, he will become a Syrian problem and not a
> Lebanese problem…Let him join the Lebanese army or the Progressive
> Socialist Party…There are Arab countries that pay for him Libya does not
> mind the loss of a few million, but it is difficult to have an army at the
> Syrian border.[52]

Clearly, the Syrian regime would allow neither the PLO nor another Arab country to

interfere in achieving their goals. The Khatib defection, along with renewed offensive

actions by National Movement forces, convinced Assad that a change in strategy was

---

[50]   Rabinovich, 50-52.

[51]   Khazen, 332-333.

[52]   Khazen, 335. By the end of the year, the LAA had virtually disappeared.

needed. He ordered Sa'iqa and PLA units to defend President Faranjiyya, thus pitting Palestinians against Palestinians.

Complimenting his military maneuvering, Assad continued to shape the battlefield diplomatically. In late March, U.S. envoy Dean Brown arrived in Lebanon. In his report to Secretary of State Henry Kissinger, Brown gave his assurance that Lebanon was in no danger of becoming a Syrian satellite.[53] For his part, Kissinger was more than happy to let Assad solve the crisis any way he could. Kissinger felt that Syrian concentration on the Lebanese crisis would distract them from interfering in the continued reconciliation of Egypt and Israel. Kissinger convinced the Israeli's to agree to overt Syrian actions, so long as they stayed north of the Beirut-Damascus Highway and refrained from bringing in Surface to Air Missiles.[54]

Likewise, Assad began shaping opinion to accept the new strategy he was undoubtedly contemplating. On April 10th, the Lebanese Constitution was amended to allow for an early election of President, which would enable Assad to move Elyas Sarkis into power. This was accompanied by movement of Syrian army regular troops into eastern Lebanon.[55] Two days later, he publicly denounced the National Movement, blaming them for continued fighting and undermining the peace efforts. This speech was largely directed at other Arab nations, preparing them for the apparent shift in allegiance that was soon to come. On 12 May, Sarkis was elected President, and war moved into its fourth phase.

---

[53]   Deeb, 132.

[54]   Seale, 278-280.

[55]   Deeb, 130.

Phase IV-Full Military Intervention

With his inability to achieve his goal of ending the war with conditions in his favor, Assad decided to use regular forces, and the overt invasion of Lebanon began. Assad's aim was now to defeat the leftist forces that threatened to defeat the Christians, upsetting Assad's goals. The Syrians had four tactical goals. First was to separate the PLO from the central Lebanon Shuf area, dividing them from the National Movement stronghold and pushing them back to the camps in the south. Second was the restoration of the Christians to their traditional territory around Mount Lebanon. Third was to defeat the reformists around Tripoli. And finally, was to pacify the northern and eastern parts of the country.

On May 31, Assad launched his first offensive against the National Movement. 2,000 men and 60 tanks split into three columns. One column moved south through the Bekaa Valley then across the Shuf towards Sidon, where it was halted by PLO forces. Another column moved west along the Beirut /Damascus highway stopping outside Beirut. The last column moved north through the Bekaa Valley then west to join Syrian forces around Tripoli.[56] The first offensive met with tactical failure on all fronts. Leftist forces in Mount Lebanon area and Tripoli inflicted heavy casualties on the Syrian forces. The PLO stronghold of Sidon was attacked with the same results. To complicate the problem, the Christian forces used the opportunity to lay siege to the Palestinian refugee camp of Tel al- Za'tar, which lay between Mount Lebanon and East Beirut.[57]

---

[56]   Lawerence L. Whetten, "The Military Dimension," in *Lebanon in Crisis,* eds. P. Edward Haley and Lewis W. Snider (Syracuse, NY: Syracuse University Press, 1979) 79.

[57]   Harris, 165-166.

More important than the tactical failure to defeat the leftists was the backlash among Arab nations. Syria's actions were condemned by virtually all, and Assad once again launched a political campaign to explain his motives. Foreign Minister Khaddam was dispatched to the USSR on July 5-8, and other envoys visited North African nations to explain the Syrian position.[58] On July 20th, Assad gave a speech to the Syrian public, a message meant for a much larger audience. In it, he explained that the PLO had deviated from their goal, and had abandoned the Palestinian cause by getting involved in Lebanese internal affairs. He claimed that it was the Syrian's who had remained true to the ideals of the Palestinians. In essence, he blamed the continued conflict on the PLO.[59]

Having pushed the leftist forces back into their enclaves, the summer months were typified by slow gains by the Syrians and Christians. Around the Christian city of Zahle, the Syrians and Phalangists coordinated a two pronged attack, with the Christians attacking from the west, and the Syrians the east. This scattered the besieging forces and freed the trapped Christians. Similar tactics would be used around Tripoli. In the south, the Syrians ran into more trouble. The Palestinians had adjusted to fighting against tanks, which were restricted to the roads. The Syrians lost many tanks and shifted tactics. Tanks joined artillery as fire support platforms, supporting infantry advances. These tactics significantly reduced losses.[60]

In September, the Christian's consolidated the militias in East Beirut into the Lebanese Forces, under Bashir Jumayyil, with the political wing being called the

---

[58]   Deeb, 135.

[59]   Deeb 135.

[60]   Whetten, 80.

Lebanese Front, under Camille Chamoun. These actions enraged the Sunni majority, who already saw the joint Syrian/Christian action as collusion between two minority sects, the Alawis and the Christians.[61] By this time, however, the leftist forces were losing ground. The Amal militia and many of the Sunni organizations accepted Syrian terms, leaving only the PLO and the remnants of the National Movement. In their final attack, the Syrians pushed out of Zahle along three columns towards Beirut, Tripoli, and Jezzine, near Sidon. Unlike their earlier actions, this time 15,000 additional men were included.[62] By October the end was in sight for the PLO. Here, once again, events took a twist.[63]

Between October 16-18, with the PLO on the verge of collapse, Assad attended the Six Parties Summit in Riyad. At the summit, it was decided that a cease-fire with an occupying Arab Deterrence Force (ADF) was needed to end the crisis. The participants accepted and legitimized the Syrian forces already in Lebanon as the core of the ADF. It would remain almost exclusively Syrian.[64]

Assad walked away from the conference having attained virtually all his operational goals and some of his strategic ones. He had control of the Beirut-Damascus Highway. A government decidedly pro-Syrian was in place, and his actions in Lebanon removed the immediate threat of a destabilizing regime. He had pushed the PLO back into their camps, although the complete control he had sought eluded him. Assad felt he had gained acceptance as the pan-Arabist leader by virtue of the Syrian assignment as the

---

[61]   Harris, 166.

[62]   Deeb, 81.

[63]   Harris, 166-168.

[64]   Rabinovich, 56.

core of the ADF. The Civil War ended with Assad a clear winner in his own eyes. But operational and tactical success does not mean the success of long-term strategic goals are assured, as we will see in the next chapter.

CHAPTER 4

FAILURE OF STRATEGY

If one looked at the situation in Lebanon at the end of 1976, the conclusion would have to be that Hafiz Assad had gained militarily and diplomatically. He had indeed stopped the fighting, eliminating the threat of radical inter-sectarian fighting from spilling over into Syria, which was his first strategic objective. He had eliminated the threat of Israeli intervention and controlled the strategic Bekaa valley, which was his second objective. He had subdued, if not totally gained control of, the Palestinian Liberation Organization, and was in a position to exert state sponsorship, which achieved his third aim. Assad had gained Arab approval of his forces in Lebanon under the guise of the Arab Deterrent Force, gaining acceptance as a regional power and giving him some legitimacy as the new leader of pan-Arabism. And he was well positioned to achieve his goal of a "Greater Syria." But as we will see, conflicting strategic aims and misapplied force contributed to continued strife, costly occupation, and an inability to achieve all of his long term goals.

Rather than provide for security, the mismatch, or possibly incompleteness of Assad's operational goals led to continued conflict and threatened to topple his regime. First, the Syrian intervention did not stop the violence for long. As author Harry N. Howard states

> But the fighting did not entirely cease, even though it was not on a scale
> comparable to the conflict which had taken place during some nineteen

months in 1975-76. Tensions persisted, particularly in south Lebanon, despite the cease-fire which had gone into effect in November 1976.[65]

In fact the violence in Lebanon would continue for another 14 years, finally ending in 1990 when the Syrians, with full backing of the United States, rolled into the Presidential Palace and toppled Michael Aoun's resistance to Syrian hegemony.[66]

Second, while Syria was targeting the radical movements within Lebanon, inside Syria itself radical forces were gaining momentum. By the late 1970's, with Assad preoccupied with foreign affairs, dissatisfaction at home over economic malaise and Assad's perceived neglect of domestic affairs emboldened the Moslem Brotherhood to begin terrorist acts on a large scale in Syria.[67] The Brotherhood was covertly supported by elements within Lebanon who provided safe havens and arms to the guerillas.[68] Between 1979 and 1982, Assad was preoccupied with fighting against the Moslem Brotherhood, which seriously threatened his regime. Thus, the Syrian excursion into Lebanon unleashed the very forces Assad had hoped to quell.

Syria failed to achieve their goal, extending rather than stopping the violence. As stated earlier, one of the Syrian operational objectives was to separate the PLO from the Christian region and drive them into the camps. While certainly a militarily achievable objective, it did nothing to alleviate the underlying tensions that had caused the war to begin with. All the Syrians had accomplished was to essentially restore the *status quo*

---

[65]   Harry N. Howard,."The United Nations and the Arab League," in *Lebanon in Crisis*, eds. P. Edward Haley and Lewis W. Snider (Syracuse, NY: Syracuse University Press, 1979), 282.

[66]   Harris, 277.

[67]   Seale, 317.

[68]   Seale, 336.

ante bellum. To exploit their success, Syria needed a comprehensive plan to resolve the social tensions that caused the war in the beginning, a political endstate that was probably unattainable at the time. Furthermore, Syria's continued presence after 1976 quickly alienated the Lebanese, particularly the Christians. "With the rising incidence of pillage and rape, arbitrary arrests, and confiscation of property, the country's Christian population was finding itself increasingly disenchanted with the Syrians."[69] The Christians then supported the Muslim Brotherhood against Assad. Thus, a mismatch between his first strategic objective and his operational military goal prevented Assad from meeting his aim.

Assad's biggest fear was Israeli intervention in Lebanon, and hence encirclement of Syria, yet his own operations ultimately did nothing to stop the Israelis from twice sending incursions of their own. First in March, 1978, Operation *Litani* was launched to drive the PLO back across the Litani river. The PLO's continued harassment of northern Israeli settlements had to be stopped, and Operation *Litani* was supposed to drive the PLO north of the Litani River where their artillery could not fire into Israel. Syria could do nothing as the Israelis moved in and the PLO fled north. The operation was a failure as the PLO simply moved back as the Israeli's withdrew, but it should have signaled to the Syrian President a willingness of Israel to send forces into Lebanon.

Israel again attacked in June, 1982 with the goal of destroying the PLO once and for all, pushing the Syrians out of Lebanon, and achieving recognition by the Lebanese government.[70] The inclusion of direct actions against the Syrians as a goal shows how

---

[69]   Ze'ev Schiff and Ehud Ya'ari, *Israel's Lebanon War* (New York, NY: Simon and Schuster, 1984), 23.

[70]   Schiff and Ya'ri, 42.

their very presence there, rather than deterring the Israelis, was in fact a provocation to them. The Israelis would maintain a military presence in Lebanon for the next 20 years.

It appears from the foregoing that Assad failed to achieve his second strategic goal. This was not just a case of unintended consequences of the prolonged Syrian presence, although their presence was largely responsible. The Syrian failure to disarm the militias led to continued Syrian military presence, which pushed the Christians to more closely ally themselves with the Israelis. This alliance eventually brought Israeli intervention. Furthermore, Assad's desire to have unilateral control over the fate of Lebanon, his "Greater Syria" vision, was perceived by the Israelis as a block to meeting their own strategic aims. They could not gain recognition from Lebanon if the Syrians were there. Thus the Syrian strategic goals of a Greater Syria and preventing Israeli intervention conflicted with each other. However, it was Assad's failure to restrain PLO actions that ultimately forced the Israelis to act.

Assad failed to achieve his third goal of controlling the PLO for several reasons. After successfully pushing the PLO back into the camps in 1976, Assad was stymied at the Riyad conference in October of that year. While Syria successfully gained acceptance as the lead nation of the Arab Deterrent Force in Lebanon, one of the stipulations of the conference was the reinstatement of the terms of the 1969 Cairo Agreement, which had given the PLO virtual autonomy in the south of Lebanon. [71] The Syrians did disarm the PLO to a certain degree, but within a couple years they were once again armed with heavy weapons. Assad, distracted by domestic events, could do nothing about it.

---

[71]   Rabinovich, 56.

Keeping in mind that Assad also wanted to gain acceptance as the leader of pan-Arabic sentiment, it is hard to imagine that he could crush the PLO, the perceived leader of the Palestinian movement, and weather the criticism that was bound to come from within Syria and the Arab world at large. Assad did in fact come under tremendous pressure for supporting the Phalangists against the PLO.[72] These attacks led him to give a landmark speech to the people of Syria, in essence explaining that Arafat had abrogated his right to claim leadership of the Palestinian cause by meddling in Lebanese politics, which had nothing to do with the fight against Israel.[73] From 1976-1984, Assad continued to fight against Arafat, both directly and by proxy, until the Israeli's succeeded in expelling the PLO from Lebanon. However, he was never able to gain the mantle as the leader of the Palestinians, and Arafat retains that position today.

Assad had hoped to use the Lebanese experience to bolster his claim as the leader of Pan-Arabism. His military actions, however, failed entirely to support that claim. First, as has been noted, his support of the Phalangist Christians against the PLO earned him considerable retribution at home and throughout the Arab world. "The Lion of Arabism was slaughtering Arabism's sacred cow. For the rest of his presidency Assad was to bear the burden of a policy which was as unpopular with the Arab masses as it was misunderstood."[74] Instead of supporting his claim as Gamal Nasser's successor, Assad's misuse of military means to gain a strategic end prevented him from ever reaching his goal.

---

[72]   Harris, 166.

[73]   Rabinovich, 183-218.

[74]   Seale, 285.

One other factor relating to Lebanon that seemed to go against his claim was Assad's insistence on unilateral action. On October 15, 1975, the Arab League held a meeting to discuss the Lebanese crisis. Syria boycotted the meeting. To Assad, "…no Arab country had the right to discuss the security and stability of Lebanon except Syria."[75] This shortsightedness certainly was not a pan-Arabic sentiment, and Assad lost an opportunity to give the appearance of international action to the events that followed.

One of the ironies of Syria's military intervention in Lebanon is that, of the five strategic goals, achieving his vision of Lebanon as an integral part of Syria is the most controversial, and is paradoxically the one he came closest to achieving. The evidence is overwhelming that Assad saw Lebanon as a *de facto* Syrian state. Authors Itamar Rabinovich[76] and Martha Kessler,[77] however, both argue that a "Greater Syria" was not a goal of Assad. Author William Harris disagrees and makes the point that it was part of Assad's long term vision.[78] Regardless if it was an initial goal in Lebanon or not, Assad certainly capitalized on his position to work towards eventual integration.

The near achievement of his goal to integrate Lebanon had its roots in his initial intervention in the Lebanese civil war. First, Assad was willing to bear the expense and the brunt of criticism against his long occupation. Second, from 1976-1989 when the Ta'if Accord was signed, legitimizing Syria's actions in Lebanon, Assad deftly manipulated the various factions against one another. He correctly saw the critical

---

[75]   Deeb, 125.

[76]   Rabinovich, 48.

[77]   Martha Neff Kessler, *Syria: Fragile Mosaic of Power* (Washington, DC: National Defense University Press, 1987) 57-58.

[78]   Harris, 275, 278. Harris uses the terms hegemony and Syrianization, but the intent is the same.

vulnerability of the Lebanese as their inability to put sectarian differences aside long enough to consolidate against him. Thus at various time, he pitted Shi'i against Palestinian, Christian against Shi'i, Palestinian against Palestinian, or virtually any other combination of faction against faction.

While Assad was able to establish hegemony over Lebanon over time, challenges to Syria's continued status in Lebanon still exist. First, the withdrawl of Israel forces from southern Lebanon has exposed the Syrian occupation for what it is…an occupation by foreign forces for their own ends. The Syrians can no longer use the Israeli presence to justify their military existence in Lebanon. Second there is evidence that the occupying force has worn out their welcome with Muslim as well as Christians in Lebanon. At a 1997 all-star soccer game between the Syrians and Lebanese, a crowd of mostly Muslim Lebanese fans called for the withdrawl of Syrian forces. In 1999, students were arrested for handing out leaflets that called for Syria to leave, and in 2000, a crowd protested in front of the Justice Ministry. Even newspapers are starting to print anti-Syrian articles. [79] It remains to be seen whether "Greater Syria" becomes a reality or not.

Having seen how Syrian strategic and operational goals were unattainable, it is useful to analyze the Syrian actions from an American viewpoint. This approach is key to understanding fully Assad's dilemma in Lebanon.

---

[79]   Pipes, PP 24-25

CHAPTER 5

ASSAD AND THE POWELL DOCTRINE

This chapter will analyze Assad's strategy in Lebanon with the "Powell Doctrine." While he was Chairman of the Joint Chiefs of Staff, General Colin Powell stated his views on the conditions that should exist before military force is used. The "Powell Doctrine" as it has been coined contains the following elements concerning the use of military force. Is there a clearly defined goal? Is the military able to achieve that goal? Have all other means to achieve that goal been attempted before we commit forces? What costs will be incurred? What are the risks and gains? What are the consequences of our actions? Powell went on to add that once military force is decided on, it should be used decisively.

Powell's ideas on the use of military force are useful in analyzing the Syrian intervention in Lebanon. Assad's goals have already been discussed, but what about the rest of the doctrine? What were the costs of intervention? Did Assad exhaust all other means before military force was committed? Did the Syrian President adequately weigh the risks against the gains? Was decisive military force used? These questions will be answered in turn.

Economically, the cost of intervention for Syria was a high one. About eighteen percent of Syria's Gross Domestic Product was going to military expenditures during that time frame. Had Assad been willing or able to extricate himself from Lebanon, the impact of the intervention would have been negligible. As it turned out, Syria was to stay in Lebanon, and the drain on the Syrian society was high. To exacerbate the problem, the oil states that had subsidized Assad since the October War cut back their subsidies in protest of his actions against the PLO.[80] In 1976, then, the economic impact was decidedly negative, but it paled in comparison to the political costs to Assad.

Assad paid a heavy political price for fighting against the PLO. Pro-PLO protests occurred at Syrian embassies in many countries. He forfeited his claim as the Pan-Arab leader. Relations with the Soviet Union, his prime military benefactor, became decidedly cool. Syria would not receive another shipment of arms from Russia until 1978.[81] Among the other Arab states, Assad's involvement in Lebanon caused them to be nervous as Syria's prominence in the region rose and traditional regional rivalries entered the scene.[82] But the greatest price paid by Assad was the unleashing of domestic dissent within Syria itself, where the unpopularity of his actions, along with an influx of Lebanese refugees into the cities, exacerbated the tensions that led to his eventual showdown with the Muslim Brotherhood.

Military action was not the first option for Assad. The Syrians did try other means to achieve their goals. Diplomatically, they attempted to get the combatants to come to agreement several times, but the cease fires were always temporary. By shutting out the other Arab League nations from the process, however, Assad failed to capitalize on an opportunity to truly meet his goals. Had the combined leaders of the Arab states threatened Arafat, Jumblatt and the reformists that they would all intervene if the fighting

---

[80]   Seale, 285.

[81]   Seale, 287.

did not cease, it is highly unlikely that some diplomatic solution would not have been found. In fact, had a true Arab coalition force been formed, Assad could have prevented the problems he faced later by acting unilaterally. Instead he found himself in a quagmire from which he could not escape and ensured that Syria alone was to blame for the ensuing years of conflict.

From the foregoing, it is clear that Assad grossly underestimated the risks involved in his conducting military excursions, particularly against the PLO who were supported by all the Arab states as well as his Soviet supporters. Concern about Israeli intervention coupled with Assad's other long term goals in Lebanon blinded him to a close analysis of the unintended consequences of his actions, hence the backlash among the Arab states and in Syria. He had a lot to gain, if he was successful, but he risked a tremendous amount on his intervention, and ultimately failed due to poor risk analysis. Having failed to use all diplomatic venues available to him, and having failed to adequately weigh the costs, risk, and gains, Assad decided to use military force.

Syria had a military capable of defeating anything the Lebanese militias could muster. The officers were loyal and combat experienced. They were better equipped and were potentially facing fractured groups that could be defeated one by one. But the internal security needs and threat from Iraq limited his ability to muster overwhelming force. The 35,000 troops he eventually sent in were spread thin throughout Lebanon, occupying areas throughout the country instead of concentrating at the critical area around Beirut and the PLO camps. His forces were sufficient to separate the PLO from the Christian area and at least temporarily bring conflict termination, but were not enough to enforce the disarmament of the militias prescribed by the Riyad Conference. To

---

[82]   Seale, 294.

achieve a lasting peace, the Syrians needed to decisively defeat the militias and achieve conditions for conflict resolution, which Assad failed to do.

By not fully following the Powell Doctrine, Assad lost an opportunity to quickly achieve his strategic objectives. He did not adequately weigh the costs against the benefits, for which he paid a high price economically and politically. He failed to exploit diplomatic opportunities by excluding other Arab nations from the process. And he did not apply decisive force at the times and places when it was needed. We turn now to the implications for United States warfighters.

CHAPTER 6

KEY JUDGEMENTS AND CONCLUSIONS

The previous chapters have shown how Assad failed or only partially achieved his long-range strategic objectives in Lebanon. He failed to gain control of the PLO or to achieve the leadership of the Arab states. Syria's presence in Lebanon brought him in direct confrontation with Israel at a time when he desperately wanted to avoid it, and resulted in twenty years of Israeli presence in southern Lebanon. While there has been limited success in achieving a "Greater Syria," the extent to which that goal will ultimately be achieved is yet to be defined. Finally, he achieved some semblance of peace on his western border, but that peace is based on continued occupation that is not only destroying the fabric of Lebanon, but is still fragile.

The reasons for Assad's failure to gain his objectives have been demonstrated in the previous chapters. Broadly speaking, they can be summarized as: (1) a failure to foresee the domestic implications of foreign intervention; (2) a failure to gain a coalition to achieve his goals in Lebanon; (3) a tendency to rely too much on military means to achieve his goals; (4) a failure to use decisive military force once committed, and finally; (5) pursuing conflicting strategic interests. How these lessons apply to the United States will be explored below. While there are no new lessons learned, the conclusions drawn from Assad's mistakes are nevertheless useful.

The link between domestic and international affairs is perhaps more applicable to the United States today than it was to Syria in 1976. The "CNN Factor" places a big burden on warfighters and must be an integral factor in planning and conducting military operations in the far reaches of the globe. Assad suffered severely for failing to satisfactorily explain his reasons for intervention on behalf of the Christians. It is incumbent upon the military leaders today to provide military options that are palatable to the American public. Like it or not, the media will be a part of every foreign operation in the future, and the lesson of Lebanon is that a failure to take domestic concerns into account is a failure of the operational art.

Another valuable lesson that the Syrian experience highlights is the usefulness of coalition operations. As the sole superpower of the world, unilateral action by the United States can be easily interpreted as heavy-handed bullying. Coalition forces not only add a sense of legitimacy to our actions, but can also help us avoid choosing actions that may have unintended consequences due to our cultural ignorance. They can, in essence, provide a different set of values to our proposed actions and provide feedback on the likely regional reactions to the plan. Finally, coalition endorsement of U.S. actions provides political pressure on the target country. Had Assad incorporated the other Arab states, the concerted political pressure may have diplomatically forced the PLO to withdraw from the Christian enclave, and found a peaceful solution to the crisis.

The tendency to rely too much on the military as a means to achieve a desired end with a resulting inability to disengage is paralleled by the United States today and Assad's Syria of 1976. The United States is presently engaged in a war against terrorists in Afghanistan. Militarily, it has been a huge success so far, but it is increasingly evident that American forces will have to remain for some time to come to prevent a resurgence of terrorist cells in the future. Assad faced the same problem in Lebanon. It was easy to get in, but nearly impossible for him to get out. Military force is best used alongside economic and diplomatic efforts. Conflict termination must include conflict resolution to be effective.

When Assad committed military force, he did so in a piecemeal fashion, first by trying to accomplish his aims with the Syrian backed Palestinian units, then committing too few troops to accomplish the mission. He at last had to send in a large contingent that ended the immediate fighting. Even then, the forces assigned were insufficient to disarm the militias or the PLO, with the resulting turmoil throughout the next 15 years. Had decisive force been used by Assad to eliminate or minimize the armed threat in the country, he would have created conditions for the army to become an instrument of state power, instead of just one of many armed groups, unable to impose their will on the other groups. Force, when used, is most effective when applied overwhelmingly to defeat the enemy's will. Assad failed to defeat the will of the factional groups.

Finally, Assad's experience reinforces the notion that good operational and tactical art cannot overcome poor or conflicting strategies. Assad's long-term goals were compromised by his inability to reconcile his goals in Lebanon with his competing long-term strategic interests. By fighting against the PLO, he isolated himself from the other Arab nations and alienated his Soviet benefactors. As a superpower with worldwide strategic interests, the United States today can easily fall into the same trap. The American experience in Somalia in 1991-93 conforms to this model. Our inability to separate strategic interests from a regional conflict with little strategic implications ultimately led to the humiliating withdrawl of American forces from the region. Relying too much on military means without successful diplomatic initiatives to complement the military cost the U.S. politically and economically. All elements of national power must be employed.

One has to wonder whether Assad would have changed his mind about intervening in Lebanon had he known that his initial intervention would lead to twenty-six years of continued occupation. On the other hand, it may have been worth the gamble to him. After all, reunifying Lebanon and Syria had been a part of his goal, and his willingness to sustain a presence for over twenty-six years earned him *de facto* if not *de jure* control over the country. It appears that this strategic goal was worth enough to the Syrian President to risk the cost of occupation.

Understanding the key lessons of the Syrian intervention in Lebanon and their application to the United States today, some recommendations for the future can be given. In looking at the future, the United States must guard against getting bogged down in long term military occupation. Our relative overwhelming military power and inherent national impatience can easily lead us to believe that the military gains we make are obtaining our long-term goals. The true test of military operations, however, is not whether they solve the immediate crisis, but how well they pave the way for conflict resolution and solving the underlying problems of the crisis.

With worldwide commitments and interests, the United States is today facing problems that simply cannot be solved without assistance from our allies. The temptation to act unilaterally may at times be extremely tempting. But allied forces add a legitimacy to actions that should not be overlooked, as well as the crucial addition of military power. Whenever possible, United Nations approval for American actions should be sought. When circumstances prohibit timely United Nations actions, multilateral endorsements need to be promoted. By doing so, the United States will better balance short term objectives with long term strategic aims.

Throughout the world, the regional instability found in 1975-76 Lebanon still exists. Whether conflict stems from radical religious movements, ethnic conflicts, or ideological based factionalism, American forces will continue to confront cultures significantly different from our own. To operate in those environments, we must continue to develop a better understanding of the underlying issues that affect the regions we operate in. One must ask, if Syria, which has common language, common bonds, and common religion with the Lebanese, could not easily impose its will on its weaker neighbor, how can we, with our alien culture, best engage the nations of the world to our benefit?

A relatively small investment in resources can provide one answer to mitigate the problem. Deploying Marine Expeditionary Units often call on regional experts to brief cultural issues to their personnel. This program can be enlarged to include briefs to other operational units. The time spent on understanding fundamental cultural issues can prevent problems from occurring during operations, and would assist operational warplanners in understanding the consequences of the actions they are contemplating.

America holds a unique position in the world today as the only superpower. But historically, the world conditions that allow for dominance by one nation are short lived. It is against America's best interests to assume that the position of dominance held today will remain indefinitely. An over-reliance on military power has resulted in American forces being engaged virtually across the world. The dangers of strategic overreach, particularly when homeland defense has placed new demands on the military, exists today to a greater level than ever before. Is a large force structure in Europe still needed? Are the forces in Asia still required on the same scale? Are these forces better utilized in those theaters or could they be better utilized for homeland defense? Military planners will have to carefully weigh the requirements of the future and answer these questions.

The lessons of Syrian intervention in Lebanon cannot be discounted. Military force is a key element of national power, but it is limited. The military is best used when providing security and reducing conflict between warring factions, tasks where the training and technology can be brought to bear. And that force is best utilized when applied alongside that of our allies. But extended occupation has price that can often be counterproductive to long term strategic goals. It is a lesson we cannot afford to forget.

APPENDIX A: THE ALAWI RELIGION

The Alawi are a secretive Muslim sect with many heterodox practices that make them suspected by more conservative Muslims. Many of their beliefs are known only to the initiated. While they believe in the five pillars of Islam, they do not pray in mosques, holding no building as more sacred than any other. The Alawis believe in a trinity, the divinity of Ali, and celebrate Easter, Christmas, and Epiphany.[83]

During the French Mandate, the French recruited heavily among minority groups to counter Sunni power. The Alawis found upward mobility in the armed forces after years of persecution, both direct and indirect. Thus the army had a disproportionate number of Alawi officers in it.

Not surprisingly, Assad's strength of his ties with the army was in many ways traced to his religious affiliation. Although not exclusively, his closest advisors were Alawis. Thus, the Sunni majority always remained somewhat suspicious of an Alawi conspiracy.

---

[83]   Tomas Collelo ed., *Syria: A Country Study*, 3rd ed., Federal Research Division, Library of Congress, DA Pam. No. 550-47 (Washington, DC: GPO, 1988), 96-97.

NOTE: MAP OMITTED DUE TO DISK SIZE CONSTRAINTS

MAP 1. Lebanon

Source: URL: http://www.lib.utexas.edu/maps/middle_east_and_asia>, accessed
6April, 2002.

BIBLIOGRAPHY

Burch, John C., CDR, USN. *BackGround Issues Concerning Soviet Foreign Policy and Syrian Initiatives in the Middle East*. Naval PostGraduate Thesis. Monterey: Naval PostGraduate School, March, 1986.

Collelo Tomas, ed., *Syria: A Country Study*, 3rd ed. Federal Research Division, Library of Congress, DA Pam. No. 550-47. Washington, DC: GPO, 1988.

Deeb, Marius. *The Lebanese Civil War*. New York: Praeger Publishers, 1980.

Harris, William W. *Faces of Lebanon*. Princeton: Markus Weiner Publishers, 1996.

Huber, Mark A., LT, USN. *Legitimacy and Hafez Al-Asad*. Naval Postgraduate School Thesis. Monterey: Naval Postgraduate School, June, 1992.

Kessler, Martha Neff. *Syria: Fragile Mosaic of Power*. Washington, DC: National Defense University Press, 1987.

Khazen, Farid El. The Breakdown of the State of Lebanon 1967-1976. Cambridge: 2000.

Lebanon in Crisis. Eds. P. Edward Haley and Lewis W. Snider. Syracuse: Syracuse University Press, 1979.

Malik, Habib C. "Is There Still a Lebanon?" *Middle East Quarterly*, December, 1997.

Mugraby, Muhammed, "Lebanon, a Wholly Owned Subsidiary," *Middle East Quarterly*, March 1998.

Pipes, Daniel. "We Don't Need Syria in Lebanon." *Middle East Quarterly*, September 2000.

Rabinovich, Itamar. *The War for Lebanon 1970-1983*. Ithaca: Cornell University Press, 1984.

Schiff, Ze'ev and Ehud Ya'ari. *Israel's Lebanon War*. New York: Simon and Schuster, 1984.

Seale, Patrick. *ASAD of Syria: The Struggle for the Middle East.* London: I. B. Tauris & Co Ltd, 1988.

Talhami, Ghada H. *Syria and the Palestinians.* Gainesville: University Press of Florida, 2001.

www.ingramcontent.com/pod-product-compliance
Lightning Source LLC
Chambersburg PA
CBHW080612290526

45790CB00007B/2748